To a Skylark

PERCY BYSSHE SHELLEY

D1324292

A Phoenix Paperback

Poems and Prose by Percy Bysshe Shelley first published
by J. M. Dent in 1995

This abridged edition published in 1996 by Phoenix,
a Division of Orion Books Ltd,
Orion House, 5 Upper St Martin's Lane, London WC2H 9EA

Cover illustration: *Cornfield in Surrey*, by William Linnell,
Wolverhampton Art Galleries (Bridgeman Art Library, London)

ISBN 1 85799 674 7

Typeset by CentraCet Ltd, Cambridge
Printed in Great Britain by
Clays Ltd, St Ives plc

CONTENTS

Ozymandias

I met a traveller from an antique land
Who said: 'Two vast and trunkless legs of stone
Stand in the desert. Near them, on the sand,
Half sunk, a shattered visage lies, whose frown,
And wrinkled lip, and sneer of cold command,
Tell that its sculptor well those passions read
Which yet survive, stamped on these lifeless things,
The hand that mocked them and the heart that fed;
And on the pedestal these words appear:
"My name is Ozymandias, king of kings:
Look on my works, ye Mighty, and despair!"
Nothing beside remains. Round the decay
Of that colossal wreck, boundless and bare
The lone and level sands stretch far away.'

From *The Mask of Anarchy*
Written on The Occasion of The
Massacre at Manchester

As I lay asleep in Italy
There came a voice from over the Sea,
And with great power it forth led me
To walk in the Visions of Poesy.

I met Murder on the way –
He had a mask like Castlereagh,
Very smooth he looked, yet grim;
Seven bloodhounds followed him:

All were fat; and well they might
Be in admirable plight,
For one by one, and two by two,
He tossed them human hearts to chew
Which from his wide cloak he drew.

Next came Fraud, and he had on,
Like Eldon, an ermined gown;
His big tears, for he wept well,
Turned to mill-stones as they fell,

And the little children who
Round his feet played to and fro,

Thinking every tear a gem,
Had their brains knocked out by them.

Clothed with the Bible, as with light,
And the shadows of the night,
Like Sidmouth next, Hypocrisy
On a crocodile rode by.

And many more Destructions played
In this ghastly masquerade,
All disguised, even to the eyes,
Like Bishops, lawyers, peers or spies.

Last came Anarchy: he rode
On a white horse, splashed with blood;
He was pale even to the lips,
Like Death in the Apocalypse.

And he wore a kingly crown;
And in his grasp a sceptre shone;
On his brow this mark I saw –
'I AM GOD AND KING AND LAW.'

With a pace stately and fast,
Over English land he passed,
Trampling to a mire of blood
The adoring multitude.

And a mighty troop around,
With their trampling shook the ground,
Waving each a bloody sword,
For the service of their Lord;

And with glorious triumph, they
Rode through England proud and gay,
Drunk as with intoxication
Of the wine of desolation.

O'er fields and towns, from sea to sea,
Passed that Pageant swift and free,
Tearing up and trampling down
Till they came to London town;

And each dweller, panic-stricken,
Felt his heart with terror sicken
Hearing the tempestuous cry
Of the triumph of Anarchy.

For with pomp to meet him came
Clothed in arms like blood and flame
The hired Murderers, who did sing
'Thou art God and Law and King.

'We have waited weak and lone
For thy coming, Mighty One!

Our purses are empty, our swords are cold,
Give us glory and blood and gold.'

Lawyers and priests, a motley crowd,
To the Earth their pale brows bowed,
Like a bad prayer not overloud
Whispering – 'Thou art Law and God.'

Then all cried with one accord
'Thou art King and God and Lord;
Anarchy, to Thee we bow,
Be Thy name made holy now!'

And Anarchy, the Skeleton,
Bowed and grinned to every one,
As well as if his education
Had cost ten millions to the Nation.

For he knew the Palaces
Of our Kings were rightly his;
His the sceptre, crown and globe,
And the gold-inwoven robe.

So he sent his slaves before
To seize upon the Bank and Tower,
And was proceeding with intent
To meet his pensioned Parliament

When One fled past, a Maniac maid,
And her name was Hope, she said:
But she looked more like Despair,
And she cried out in the air –

'My father Time is weak and grey
With waiting for a better day –
See how idiot-like he stands
Fumbling with his palsied hands!

He has had child after child
And the dust of death is piled
Over every one but me –
Misery, o Misery!'

Then she lay down in the street
Right before the horses' feet,
Expecting with a patient eye
Murder, Fraud and Anarchy,

When between her and her foes
A mist, a light, an image rose,
Small at first, and weak and frail
Like the vapour of a vale,

Till as clouds grow on the blast
Like tower-crowned giants striding fast,

And glare with lightnings as they fly
And speak in thunder to the sky,

It grew – a Shape arrayed in mail
Brighter than the viper's scale,
And upborne on wings whose grain
Was as the light of sunny rain.

On its helm seen far away
A planet, like the Morning's lay;
And those plumes its light rained through
Like a shower of crimson dew;

With step as soft as wind it passed
O'er the heads of men – so fast
That they knew the presence there
And looked – but all was empty air.

As flowers beneath May's footstep waken,
As stars from Night's loose hair are shaken,
As waves arise when loud winds call,
Thoughts sprung where'er that step did fall.

And the prostrate multitude
Looked – and ankle-deep in blood
Hope, that maiden most serene,
Was walking with a quiet mien,

And Anarchy, the ghastly birth,
Lay dead earth upon the earth –
The Horse of Death tameless as wind
Fled, and with his hoofs did grind
To dust the murderers thronged behind.

A rushing light of clouds and splendour,
A sense awakening and yet tender
Was heard and felt – and at its close
These words of joy and fear arose

As if their own indignant Earth
Which gave the Sons of England birth
Had felt their blood upon her brow,
And shuddering with a mother's throe

Had turned every drop of blood
By which her face had been bedewed
To an accent unwithstood –
As if her heart cried out aloud:

'Men of England, Heirs of Glory,
Heroes of unwritten Story,
Nurslings of one mighty Mother,
Hopes of her and one another,

'Rise like Lions after slumber
In unvanquishable number,

Shake your chains to Earth like dew
Which in sleep had fallen on you –
Ye are many – they are few.

'What is Freedom? – ye can tell
That which slavery is, too well –
For its very name has grown
To an echo of your own.

''Tis to work and have such pay
As just keeps life from day to day
In your limbs, as in a cell
For the tyrants' use to dwell,

'So that ye for them are made
Loom and plough and sword and spade,
With or without your own will bent
To their defence and nourishment;

''Tis to see your children weak
With their mothers pine and peak
When the winter winds are bleak –
They are dying whilst I speak;

''Tis to hunger for such diet
As the rich man in his riot
Casts to the fat dogs that lie
Surfeiting beneath his eye;

"Tis to let the Ghost of Gold
Take from Toil a thousandfold
More than e'er its substance could
In the tyrannies of old –

'Paper coin, that forgery
Of the title deeds, which ye
Hold to something from the worth
Of the inheritance of Earth;

"Tis to be a slave in soul
And to hold no strong control
Over your own will, but be
All that others make of ye;

'And at length when ye complain
With a murmur weak and vain,
'Tis to see the tyrants' crew
Ride over your wives and you –
Blood is on the grass like dew.

Ode to the West Wind

I

O wild West Wind, thou breath of Autumn's being,
Thou, from whose unseen presence the leaves dead
Are driven, like ghosts from an enchanter fleeing,

Yellow, and black, and pale, and hectic red,
Pestilence-stricken multitudes: O thou,
Who chariotest to their dark wintry bed

The wingèd seeds, where they lie cold and low,
Each like a corpse within its grave, until
Thine azure sister of the Spring shall blow

Her clarion o'er the dreaming earth, and fill
(Driving sweet buds like flocks to feed in air)
With living hues and odours plain and hill:

Wild Spirit, which art moving everywhere;
Destroyer and Preserver; hear, O hear!

2

Thou on whose stream, 'mid the steep sky's commotion,
Loose clouds like Earth's decaying leaves are shed,
Shook from the tangled boughs of Heaven and Ocean,

Angels of rain and lightning: there are spread
On the blue surface of thine airy surge,
Like the bright hair uplifted from the head

Of some fierce Maenad, even from the dim verge
Of the horizon to the zenith's height,
The locks of the approaching storm. Thou dirge

Of the dying year, to which this closing night
Will be the dome of a vast sepulchre
Vaulted with all thy congregated might

Of vapours, from whose solid atmosphere
Black rain, and fire, and hail will burst: O hear!

3

Thou who didst waken from his summer dreams
The blue Mediterranean, where he lay,
Lulled by the coil of his crystalline streams,

Beside a pumice isle in Baiae's bay,
And saw in sleep old palaces and towers
Quivering within the wave's intenser day,

All overgrown with azure moss and flowers
So sweet, the sense faints picturing them! Thou
For whose path the Atlantic's level powers

Cleave themselves into chasms, while far below
The sea-blooms and the oozy woods which wear
The sapless foliage of the ocean, know

Thy voice, and suddenly grow grey with fear,
And tremble and despoil themselves: O hear!

4

If I were a dead leaf thou mightest bear;
If I were a swift cloud to fly with thee;
A wave to pant beneath thy power, and share

The impulse of thy strength, only less free
Than thou, O Uncontrollable! If even
I were as in my boyhood, and could be

The comrade of thy wanderings over Heaven,
As then, when to outstrip thy skiey speed
Scarce seemed a vision; I would ne'er have striven

As thus with thee in prayer in my sore need.
Oh! lift me as a wave, a leaf, a cloud!
I fall upon the thorns of life! I bleed!

A heavy weight of hours has chained and bowed
One too like thee: tameless, and swift, and proud.

5

Make me thy lyre, even as the forest is:
What if my leaves are falling like its own!
The tumult of thy mighty harmonies

Will take from both a deep, autumnal tone,
Sweet though in sadness. Be thou, Spirit fierce,
My spirit! Be thou me, impetuous one!

Drive my dead thoughts over the universe
Like withered leaves to quicken a new birth!
And, by the incantation of this verse,

Scatter, as from an unextinguished hearth
Ashes and sparks, my words among mankind!
Be through my lips to unawakened Earth

The trumpet of a prophecy! O Wind,
If Winter comes, can Spring be far behind?

The Cloud

I bring fresh showers for the thirsting flowers,
    From the seas and the streams;
I bear light shade for the leaves when laid
    In their noon-day dreams.
From my wings are shaken the dews that waken
    The sweet buds every one,
When rocked to rest on their mother's breast,
    As she dances about the sun.
I wield the flail of the lashing hail,
    And whiten the green plains under,
And then again I dissolve it in rain,
    And laugh as I pass in thunder.

I sift the snow on the mountains below,
    And their great pines groan aghast;
And all the night 'tis my pillow white,
    While I sleep in the arms of the blast.
Sublime on the towers of my skiey bowers,
    Lightning my pilot sits,
In a cavern under is fettered the thunder,
    It struggles and howls at fits;
Over earth and ocean, with gentle motion,
    This pilot is guiding me,
Lured by the love of the genii that move
    In the depths of the purple sea;
Over the rills, and the crags, and the hills,
    Over the lakes and the plains,
Wherever he dream, under mountain or stream,
    The Spirit he loves remains;
And I all the while bask in Heaven's blue smile,
    Whilst he is dissolving in rains.

The sanguine sunrise, with his meteor eyes,
    And his burning plumes outspread,
Leaps on the back of my sailing rack,
    When the morning star shines dead;
As on the jag of a mountain crag
    Which an earthquake rocks and swings,
An eagle alit one moment may sit
    In the light of its golden wings;
And when sunset may breathe, from the lit sea beneath,

Its ardours of rest and of love,
  And the crimson pall of eve may fall
    From the depths of Heaven above,
With wings folded I rest, on mine aery nest,
    As still as a brooding dove.

That orbèd maiden with white fire laden,
    Whom mortals call the moon,
Glides glimmering o'er my fleece-like floor,
    By the midnight breezes strewn;
And wherever the beat of her unseen feet,
    Which only the angels hear,
May have broken the woof of my tent's thin roof,
    The stars peep behind her, and peer;
And I laugh to see them whirl and flee
    Like a swarm of golden bees,
When I widen the rent in my wind-built tent,
    Till the calm rivers, lakes, and seas,
Like strips of the sky fallen through me on high,
    Are each paved with the moon and these.

I bind the sun's throne with a burning zone,
    And the moon's with a girdle of pearl;
The volcanoes are dim, and the stars reel and swim,
    When the whirlwinds my banner unfurl.
From cape to cape, with a bridge-like shape,
    Over a torrent sea,
Sunbeam-proof, I hang like a roof

The mountains its columns be.
The triumphal arch through which I march
    With hurricane, fire, and snow,
When the powers of the air are chained to my chair,
    Is the million-coloured bow;
The sphere-fire above its soft colours wove,
    While the moist earth was laughing below.

I am the daughter of Earth and Water,
    And the nursling of the sky;
I pass through the pores of the oceans and shores;
    I change, but I cannot die –
For after the rain, when never a stain
    The pavilion of Heaven is bare,
And the winds and sunbeams, with their convex gleams,
    Build up the blue dome of air,
I silently laugh at my own cenotaph,
    And out of the caverns of rain,
Like a child from the womb, like a ghost from the tomb,
    I arise and unbuild it again.

The Sensitive-Plant

PART FIRST

Sensitive-plant in a garden grew,
And the young winds fed it with silver dew,
And it opened its fan-like leaves to the light
And closed them beneath the kisses of night.

And the Spring arose on the garden fair
Like the Spirit of love felt every where;
And each flower and herb on Earth's dark breast
Rose from the dreams of its wintry rest.

But none ever trembled and panted with bliss
In the garden, the field or the wilderness,
Like a doe in the noontide with love's sweet want
As the companionless Sensitive-plant.

The snowdrop and then the violet
Arose from the ground with warm rain wet,
And their breath was mixed with fresh odour, sent
From the turf, like the voice and the instrument.

Then the pied wind-flowers and the tulip tall,
And narcissi, the fairest among them all,
Who gaze on their eyes in the stream's recess
Till they die of their own dear loveliness;

And the Naiad-like lily of the vale
Whom youth makes so fair and passion so pale
That the light of its tremulous bells is seen
Through their pavilions of tender green;

And the hyacinth purple, and white, and blue,
Which flung from its bells a sweet peal anew
Of music so delicate, soft and intense,
It was felt like an odour within the sense;

And the rose like a nymph to the bath addressed,
Which unveiled the depth of her glowing breast,
Till, fold after fold, to the fainting air
The soul of her beauty and love lay bare:

And the wand-like lily, which lifted up,
As a Maenad, its moonlight-coloured cup
Till the fiery star, which is its eye,
Gazed through clear dew on the tender sky;

And the jessamine faint, and the sweet tuberose,
The sweetest flower for scent that blows;
And all rare blossoms from every clime
Grew in that garden in perfect prime.

And on the stream whose inconstant bosom
Was prankt under boughs of embowering blossom

With golden and green light, slanting through
Their heaven of many a tangled hue,

Broad water-lilies lay tremulously,
And starry river-buds glimmered by,
And around them the soft stream did glide and dance
With a motion of sweet sound and radiance.

And the sinuous paths of lawn and of moss,
Which led through the garden along and across –
Some open at once to the sun and the breeze,
Some lost among bowers of blossoming trees –

Were all paved with daisies and delicate bells
As fair as the fabulous asphodels,
And flowrets which drooping as day drooped too
Fell into pavilions, white, purple and blue,
To roof the glow-worm from the evening dew.

And from this undefiled Paradise
The flowers, as an infant's awakening eyes
Smile on its mother, whose singing sweet
Can first lull, and at last must awaken it,

When Heaven's þlithe winds had unfolded them,
As mine-lamps enkindle a hidden gem,
Shone smiling to Heaven; and every one
Shared joy in the light of the gentle sun,

For each one was interpenetrated
With the light and the odour its neighbour shed,
Like young lovers, whom youth and love make dear
Wrapped and filled by their mutual atmosphere.

But the Sensitive-plant which could give small fruit
Of the love which it felt from the leaf to the root,
Received more than all – it loved more than ever,
Where none wanted but it, could belong to the giver.

For the Sensitive-plant has no bright flower;
Radiance and odour are not its dower –
It loves – even like Love – its deep heart is full –
It desires what it has not – the beautiful!

The light winds which from unsustaining wings
Shed the music of many murmurings;
The beams which dart from many a star
Of the flowers whose hues they bear afar;

The plumèd insects swift and free
Like golden boats on a sunny sea,
Laden with light and odour, which pass
Over the gleam of the living grass;

The unseen clouds of the dew which lie
Like fire in the flowers till the Sun rides high,

Then wander like spirits among the spheres,
Each cloud faint with the fragrance it bears;

The quivering vapours of dim noontide
Which like a sea o'er the warm earth glide,
In which every sound, and odour, and beam
Move, as reeds in a single stream;

Each, and all, like ministering angels were
For the Sensitive-plant sweet joy to bear,
Whilst the lagging hours of the day went by
Like windless clouds o'er a tender sky.

And when evening descended from Heaven above,
And the Earth was all rest, and the Air was all love;
And delight, though less bright, was far more deep,
And the day's veil fell from the world of sleep,

And the beasts, and the birds, and the insects were
        drowned
In an ocean of dreams without a sound,
Whose waves never mark, though they ever impress
The light sand which paves it – Consciousness,

(Only overhead the sweet nightingale
Ever sang more sweet as the day might fail,
And snatches of its Elysian chant
Were mixed with the dreams of the Sensitive-plant)

The Sensitive-plant was the earliest
Upgathered into the bosom of rest;
A sweet child weary of its delight,
The feeblest and yet the favourite,
Cradled within the embrace of night.

Men of England: A Song

1

MEN of England, wherefore plough
For the lords who lay ye low?
Wherefore weave with toil and care
The rich robes your tyrants wear?

2

Wherefore feed and clothe and save
From the cradle to the grave,
Those ungrateful drones who would
Drain your sweat – nay, drink your blood?

3

Wherefore, Bees of England, forge
Many a weapon, chain and scourge,
That these stingless drones may spoil
The forced produce of your toil?

4

Have ye leisure, comfort, calm,
Shelter, food, love's gentle balm?
Or what is it ye buy so dear
With your pain and with your fear?

5

The seed ye sow, another reaps;
The wealth ye find, another keeps;
The robes ye weave, another wears;
The arms ye forge, another bears.

6

Sow seed – but let no tyrant reap;
Find wealth – let no impostor heap;
Weave robes – let not the idle wear;
Forge arms – in your defence to bear.

7

Shrink to your cellars, holes and cells –
In halls ye deck another dwells.
Why shake the chains ye wrought, [then] see
The steel ye tempered glance on ye.

8

With plough and spade and hoe and loom
Trace your grave and build your tomb,

And weave your winding-sheet – till fair
England be your sepulchre.

Song

Rarely, rarely, comest thou,
    Spirit of Delight!
Wherefore hast thou left me now
    Many a day and night?
Many a weary night and day
'Tis since thou art fled away.

How shall ever one like me
    Win thee back again?
With the joyous and the free
    Thou wilt scoff at pain.
Spirit false! thou hast forgot
All but those who need thee not.

As a lizard with the shade
    Of a trembling leaf,
Thou with sorrow art dismayed;
    Even the sighs of grief
Reproach thee, that thou art not near,
And reproach thou wilt not hear.

Let me set my mournful ditty
    To a merry measure;
Thou wilt never come for pity,
    Thou wilt come for pleasure;
Pity then will cut away
Those cruel wings, and thou wilt stay.

I love all that thou lovest,
    Spirit of Delight!
The fresh Earth in new leaves dressed,
    And the starry night;
Autumn evening, and the morn
When the golden mists are born.

I love snow, and all the forms
    Of the radiant frost;
I love waves and winds and storms –
    Every thing almost
Which is Nature's, and may be
Untainted by man's misery.

I love tranquil solitude,
    And such society
As is quiet, wise and good;
    Between thee and me
    What difference? – but thou dost possess
The things I seek, not love them less.

I love Love – though he has wings,
  And like light can flee
But above all other things,
  Spirit, I love thee –
Thou art Love and Life! O come,
Make once more my heart thy home.

To a Skylark

Hail to thee, blithe Spirit!
  Bird thou never wert,
That from Heaven, or near it,
  Pourest thy full heart
In profuse strains of unpremeditated art.

Higher still and higher
  From the earth thou springest
Like a cloud of fire;
  The blue deep thou wingest,
And singing still dost soar, and soaring ever singest.

In the golden lightning
  Of the sunken Sun,
O'er which clouds are bright'ning,
  Thou dost float and run;
Like an unbodied joy whose race is just begun.

The pale purple even
    Melts around thy flight;
Like a star of Heaven
    In the broad day-light
Thou art unseen, – but yet I hear thy shrill delight,

Keen as are the arrows
    Of that silver sphere
Whose intense lamp narrows
    In the white dawn clear,
Until we hardly see – we feel that it is there.

All the earth and air
    With thy voice is loud,
As when night is bare
    From one lonely cloud
The moon rains out her beams, and Heaven is
        overflowed.

What thou art we know not;
    What is most like thee?
From rainbow clouds there flow not
    Drops so bright to see,
As from thy presence showers a rain of melody.

Like a Poet hidden
    In the light of thought,
Singing hymns unbidden

Till the world is wrought
To sympathy with hopes and fears it heeded not:

Like a high-born maiden
    In a palace tower,
Soothing her love-laden
    Soul in secret hour
With music sweet as love, which overflows her bower:

Like a glow-worm golden
    In a dell of dew,
Scattering unbeholden
    Its aërial hue
Among the flowers and grass which screen it from the
        view:

Like a rose embowered
    In its own green leaves,
By warm winds deflowered,
    Till the scent it gives
Makes faint with too much sweet those heavy-wingèd
        thieves:

Sound of vernal showers
    On the twinkling grass,
Rain-awakened flowers,
    All that ever was
Joyous and clear and fresh, thy music doth surpass.

Teach us, Sprite or Bird,
    What sweet thoughts are thine;
I have never heard
    Praise of love or wine
That panted forth a flood of rapture so divine:

Chorus Hymenaeal
    Or triumphal chaunt
Matched with thine, would be all
    But an empty vaunt,
A thing wherein we feel there is some hidden want.

What objects are the fountains
    Of thy happy strain?
What fields or waves or mountains?
    What shapes of sky or plain?
What love of thine own kind? what ignorance of pain?

With thy clear keen joyance
    Languor cannot be –
Shadow of annoyance
    Never came near thee:
Thou lovest – but ne'er knew love's sad satiety.

Waking or asleep,
    Thou of death must deem
Things more true and deep

Than we mortals dream
Or how could thy notes flow in such a crystal stream?

We look before and after
    And pine for what is not:
Our sincerest laughter
    With some pain is fraught;
Our sweetest songs are those that tell of saddest thought.

Yet if we could scorn
    Hate and pride and fear;
If we were things born
    Not to shed a tear,
I know not how thy joy we ever should come near.

Better than all measures
    Of delightful sound –
Better than all treasures
    That in books are found –
Thy skill to poet were, thou scorner of the ground!

Teach me half the gladness
    That thy brain must know,
Such harmonious madness
    From my lips would flow,
The world should listen then – as I am listening now.

Adonais

I

I weep for Adonais – he is dead!
O. weep for Adonais! though our tears
Thaw not the frost which binds so dear a head!
And thou, sad Hour, selected from all years
To mourn our loss, rouse thy obscure compeers,
And teach them thine own sorrow, say: with me
Died Adonais; till the Future dares
Forget the Past, his fate and fame shall be
An echo and a light unto eternity!

2

Where wert thou, mighty Mother, when he lay,
When thy Son lay, pierced by the shaft which flies
In darkness? where was lorn Urania
When Adonais died? With veilèd eyes,
Mid listening Echoes, in her Paradise
She sate, while one, with soft enamoured breath,
Rekindled all the fading melodies
With which, like flowers that mock the corse beneath,
He had adorned and hid the coming bulk of death.

3

O, weep for Adonais – he is dead!
Wake, melancholy Mother, wake and weep!

Yet wherefore? Quench within their burning bed
Thy fiery tears, and let thy loud heart keep
Like his, a mute and uncomplaining sleep;
For he is gone, where all things wise and fair
Descend; – oh, dream not that the amorous Deep
Will yet restore him to the vital air;
Death feeds on his mute voice, and laughs at our
    despair.

4

Most musical of mourners, weep again!
Lament anew, Urania! – He died,
Who was the Sire of an immortal strain,
Blind, old, and lonely, when his country's pride
The priest, the slave, and the liberticide
Trampled and mocked with many a loathed rite
Of lust and blood; he went, unterrified,
Into the gulf of death; but his clear Sprite
Yet reigns o'er earth; the third among the sons of light.

5

Most musical of mourners, weep anew!
Not all to that bright station dared to climb;
And happier they their happiness who knew,
Whose tapers yet burn through that night of time
In which suns perished; others more sublime,
Struck by the envious wrath of man or God,
Have sunk, extinct in their refulgent prime;

And some yet live, treading the thorny road
Which leads, through toil and hate, to Fame's serene
    abode.

6

But now, thy youngest, dearest one, has perished –
The nursling of thy widowhood, who grew,
Like a pale flower by some sad maiden cherished,
And fed with true love tears, instead of dew;
Most musical of mourners, weep anew!
Thy extreme hope, the loveliest and the last,
The bloom, whose petals nipped before they blew
Died on the promise of the fruit, is waste;
The broken lily lies – the storm is overpast.

7

To that high Capital, where kingly Death
Keeps his pale court in beauty and decay,
He came; and bought, with price of purest breath,
A grave among the eternal. – Come away!
Haste, while the vault of blue Italian day
Is yet his fitting charnel-roof! while still
He lies, as if in dewy sleep he lay;
Awake him not! surely he takes his fill
Of deep and liquid rest, forgetful of all ill.

8

He will awake no more, oh, never more! –
Within the twilight chamber spreads apace
The shadow of white Death, and at the door
Invisible Corruption waits to trace
His extreme way to her dim dwelling-place;
The eternal Hunger sits, but pity and awe
Soothe her pale rage, nor dares she to deface
So fair a prey, till darkness, and the law
Of change, shall o'er his sleep the mortal curtain draw.

9

O, weep for Adonais! – The quick Dreams,
The passion-wingèd Ministers of thought,
Who were his flocks, whom near the living streams
Of his young spirit he fed, and whom he taught
The love which was its music, wander not,
Wander no more, from kindling brain to brain,
But droop there, whence they sprung; and mourn their
    lot
Round the cold heart, where, after their sweet pain,
They ne'er will gather strength, or find a home again.

10

And one with trembling hands clasps his cold head,
And fans him with her moonlight wings, and cries,
'Our love, our hope, our sorrow, is not dead;
See, on the silken fringe of his faint eyes,

Like dew upon a sleeping flower, there lies
A tear some Dream has loosened from his brain.'
Lost Angel of a ruined Paradise!
She knew not 'twas her own; as with no stain
She faded, like a cloud which had outwept its rain.

11

One from a lucid urn of starry dew
Washed his light limbs as if embalming them;
Another clipped her profuse locks, and threw
The wreath upon him, like an anadem,
Which frozen tears instead of pearls begem;
Another in her wilful grief would break
Her bow and winged reeds, as if to stem
A greater loss with one which was more weak;
And dull the barbed fire against his frozen cheek.

12

Another Splendour on his mouth alit,
That mouth, whence it was wont to draw the breath
Which gave it strength to pierce the guarded wit,
And pass into the panting heart beneath
With lightning and with music: the damp death
Quenched its caress upon his icy lips;
And, as a dying meteor stains a wreath
Of moonlight vapour, which the cold night clips,
It flushed through his pale limbs, and passed to its
        eclipse.

And others came . . . Desires and Adorations,
Wingèd Persuasions and veiled Destinies,
Splendours, and Glooms, and glimmering Incarnations
Of hopes and fears, and twilight Fantasies;
And Sorrow, with her family of Sighs,
And Pleasure, blind with tears, led by the gleam
Of her own dying smile instead of eyes,
Came in slow pomp; – the moving pomp might seem
Like pageantry of mist on an autumnal stream.

All he had loved, and moulded into thought,
From shape, and hue, and odour, and sweet sound,
Lamented Adonais. Morning sought
Her eastern watch-tower, and her hair unbound,
Wet with the tears which should adorn the ground,
Dimmed the aerial eyes that kindle day;
Afar the melancholy thunder moaned,
Pale Ocean in unquiet slumber lay,
And the wild winds flew round, sobbing in their dismay.

Lost Echo sits amid the voiceless mountains,
And feeds her grief with his remembered lay,
And will no more reply to winds or fountains,
Or amorous birds perched on the young green spray,
Or herdsman's horn, or bell at closing day,

Since she can mimic not his lips, more dear
Than those for whose disdain she pined away
Into a shadow of all sounds: – a drear
Murmur, between their songs, is all the woodmen hear.

16

Grief made the young Spring wild, and she threw down
Her kindling buds, as if she Autumn were,
Or they dead leaves; since her delight is flown,
For whom should she have waked the sullen year?
To Phoebus was not Hyacinth so dear
Nor to himself Narcissus, as to both
Thou, Adonais: wan they stand and sere
Amid the faint companions of their youth,
With dew all turned to tears; odour, to sighing ruth.

17

Thy spirit's sister, the lorn nightingale
Mourns not her mate with such melodious pain;
Not so the eagle, who like thee could scale
Heaven, and could nourish in the sun's domain
Her mighty youth with morning, doth complain,
Soaring and screaming round her empty nest,
As Albion wails for thee: the curse of Cain
Light on his head who pierced thy innocent breast,
And scared the angel soul that was its earthly guest!

18

Ah, woe is me! Winter is come and gone,
But grief returns with the revolving year;
The airs and streams renew their joyous tone;
The ants, the bees, the swallows reappear;
Fresh leaves and flowers deck the dead Season's bier;
The amorous birds now pair in every brake,
And build their mossy homes in field and brere;
And the green lizard, and the golden snake,
Like unimprisoned flames, out of their trance awake.

19

Through wood and stream and field and hill and Ocean
A quickening life from the Earth's heart has burst
As it has ever done, with change and motion,
From the great morning of the world when first
God dawned on Chaos; in its stream immersed,
The lamps of Heaven flash with a softer light;
All baser things pant with life's sacred thirst;
Diffuse themselves; and spend in love's delight
The beauty and the joy of their renewèd might.

20

The leprous corpse touched by this spirit tender
Exhales itself in flowers of gentle breath;
Like incarnations of the stars, when splendour
Is changed to fragrance, they illumine death
And mock the merry worm that wakes beneath;

Nought we know, dies. Shall that alone which knows
Be as a sword consumed before the sheath
By sightless lightning? – the intense atom glows
A moment, then is quenched in a most cold repose.

21

Alas! that all we loved of him should be,
But for our grief, as if it had not been,
And grief itself be mortal! Woe is me!
Whence are we, and why are we? of what scene
The actors or spectators? Great and mean
Meet massed in death, who lends what life must
        borrow.
As long as skies are blue, and fields are green,
Evening must usher night, night urge the morrow,
Month follow month with woe, and year wake year to
        sorrow.

22

He will awake no more, oh, never more!
'Wake thou,' cried Misery, 'childless Mother, rise
Out of they sleep, and slake, in thy heart's core,
A wound more fierce than his with tears and sighs.'
And all the Dreams that watched Urania's eyes,
And all the Echoes whom their sister's song
Had held in holy silence, cried: 'Arise!'
Swift as a Thought by the snake Memory stung,
From her ambrosial rest the fading Splendour sprung.

She rose like an autumnal Night, that springs
Out of the East, and follows wild and drear
The golden Day, which, on eternal wings,
Even as a ghost abandoning a bier,
Has left the Earth a corpse. Sorrow and fear
So struck, so roused, so rapt Urania;
So saddened round her like an atmosphere
Of stormy mist; so swept her on her way
Even to the mournful place where Adonais lay.

Out of her secret Paradise she sped,
Through camps and cities rough with stone, and steel,
And human hearts, which to her aery tread
Yielding not, wounded the invisible
Palms of her tender feet where'er they fell:
And barbèd tongues, and thoughts more sharp than they
Rent the soft Form they never could repel,
Whose sacred blood, like the young tears of May,
Paved with eternal flowers that undeserving way.

In the death-chamber for a moment Death,
Shamed by the presence of that living Might,
Blushed to annihilation, and the breath
Revisited those lips, and life's pale light
Flashed through those limbs, so late her dear delight.

'Leave me not wild and drear and comfortless,
As silent lightning leaves the starless night!
Leave me not!' cried Urania: her distress
Roused Death: Death rose and smiled, and met her vain
    caress.

26

'Stay yet awhile! speak to me once again;
Kiss me, so long but as a kiss may live;
And in my heartless breast and burning brain
That word, that kiss, shall all thoughts else survive,
With food of saddest memory kept alive,
Now thou art dead, as if it were a part
Of thee, my Adonais! I would give
All that I am to be as thou now art!
But I am chained to Time, and cannot thence depart!

27

'Oh gentle child, beautiful as thou wert,
Why didst thou leave the trodden paths of men
Too soon, and with weak hands though mighty heart
Dare the unpastured dragon in his den?
Defenceless as thou wert, oh where was then
Wisdom the mirrored shield, or scorn the spear?
Or hadst thou waited the full cycle, when
Thy spirit should have filled its crescent sphere,
The monsters of life's waste had fled from thee like deer.

'The herded wolves, bold only to pursue;
The obscene ravens, clamorous o'er the dead;
The vultures to the conqueror's banner true
Who feed where Desolation first has fed,
And whose wings rain contagion; – how they fled,
When like Apollo, from his golden bow,
The Pythian of the age one arrow sped
And smiled! – The spoilers tempt no second blow,
They fawn on the proud feet that spurn them lying low.

'The sun comes forth, and many reptiles spawn;
He sets, and each ephemeral insect then
Is gathered into death without a dawn,
And the immortal stars awake again;
So is it in the world of living men:
A godlike mind soars forth, in its delight
Making earth bare and veiling heaven, and when
It sinks, the swarms that dimmed or shared its light
Leave to its kindred lamps the spirit's awful night.'

Thus ceased she: and the mountain shepherds came,
Their garlands sere, their magic mantles rent;
The Pilgrim of Eternity, whose fame
Over his living head like Heaven is bent,
An early but enduring monument,

Came, veiling all the lightnings of his song
In sorrow; from her wilds Ierne sent
The sweetest lyrist of her saddest wrong,
And love taught grief to fall like music from his tongue.

31

Midst others of less note, came one frail Form,
A phantom among men; companionless
As the last cloud of an expiring storm
Whose thunder is its knell; he, as I guess,
Had gazed on Nature's naked loveliness,
Actaeon-like, and now he fled astray
With feeble steps o'er the world's wilderness,
And his own thoughts, along that rugged way,
Pursued, like raging hounds, their father and their
     prey.

32

A pardlike Spirit beautiful and swift –
A Love in desolation masked; – a Power
Girt round with weakness; – it can scarce uplift
The weight of the superincumbent hour;
It is a dying lamp, a falling shower,
A breaking billow; – even whilst we speak
Is it not broken? On the withering flower
The killing sun smiles brightly: on a cheek
The life can burn in blood, even while the heart may
     break.

His head was bound with pansies overblown,
And faded violets, white, and pied, and blue;
And a light spear topped with a cypress cone,
Round whose rude shaft dark ivy tresses grew
Yet dripping with the forest's noonday dew,
Vibrated, as the ever-beating heart
Shook the weak hand that grasped it; of that crew
He came the last, neglected and apart;
A herd-abandoned deer struck by the hunter's dart.

34

All stood aloof, and at his partial moan
Smiled through their tears; well knew that gentle band
Who in another's fate now wept his own –
As in the accents of an unknown land
He sung new sorrow; sad Urania scanned
The Stranger's mien, and murmured: 'Who art thou?'
He answered not, but with a sudden hand
Made bare his branded and ensanguined brow,
Which was like Cain's or Christ's – Oh! that it should be
     so!

35

What softer voice is hushed over the dead?
Athwart what brow is that dark mantle thrown?
What form leans sadly o'er the white death-bed,
In mockery of monumental stone,

The heavy heart heaving without a moan?
If it be He, who gentlest of the wise,
Taught, soothed, loved, honoured the departed one,
Let me not vex, with inharmonious sighs,
The silence of that heart's accepted sacrifice.

36

Our Adonais has drunk poison – oh!
What deaf and viperous murderer could crown
Life's early cup with such a draught of woe?
The nameless worm would now itself disown:
It felt, yet could escape, the magic tone
Whose prelude held all envy, hate, and wrong,
But what was howling in one breast alone,
Silent with expectation of the song,
Whose master's hand is cold, whose silver lyre unstrung.

37

Live thou, whose infamy is not thy fame!
Live! fear no heavier chastisement from me,
Thou noteless blot on a remembered name!
But be thyself, and know thyself to be!
And ever at thy season be thou free
To spill the venom when thy fangs o'erflow:
Remorse and Self-contempt shall cling to thee;
Hot Shame shall burn upon thy secret brow,
And like a beaten hound tremble thou shalt – as now.

Nor let us weep that our delight is fled
Far from these carrion kites that scream below;
He wakes or sleeps with the enduring dead;
Thou canst not soar where he is sitting now. –
Dust to the dust! but the pure spirit shall flow
Back to the burning fountain whence it came,
A portion of the Eternal, which must glow
Through time and change, unquenchably the same,
Whilst thy cold embers choke the sordid hearth of
    shame.

Peace, peace! he is not dead, he doth not sleep –
He hath awakened from the dream of life –
'Tis we, who lost in stormy visions, keep
With phantoms an unprofitable strife,
And in mad trance, strike with our spirit's knife
Invulnerable nothings. – *We* decay
Like corpses in a charnel; fear and grief
Convulse us and consume us day by day,
And cold hopes swarm like worms within our living
    clay.

He has outsoared the shadow of our night;
Envy and calumny and hate and pain,
And that unrest which men miscall delight,

Can touch him not and torture not again;
From the contagion of the world's slow stain
He is secure, and now can never mourn
A heart grown cold, a head grown grey in vain;
Nor, when the spirit's self has ceased to burn,
With sparkless ashes load an unlamented urn.

41

He lives, he wakes – 'tis Death is dead, not he;
Mourn not for Adonais. – Thou young Dawn
Turn all thy dew to splendour, for from thee
The spirit thou lamentest is not gone;
Ye caverns and ye forests, cease to moan!
Cease ye faint flowers and fountains, and thou Air
Which like a mourning veil thy scarf hadst thrown
O'er the abandoned Earth, now leave it bare
Even to the joyous stars which smile on its despair!

42

He is made one with Nature: there is heard
His voice in all her music, from the moan
Of thunder, to the song of night's sweet bird;
He is a presence to be felt and known
In darkness and in light, from herb and stone,
Spreading itself wherever that Power may move
Which has withdrawn his being to its own;
Which wields the world with never wearied love,
Sustains it from beneath, and kindles it above.

He is a portion of the loveliness
Which once he made more lovely: he doth bear
His part, while the one Spirit's plastic stress
Sweeps through the dull dense world, compelling there
All new successions to the forms they wear;
Torturing th'unwilling dross that checks its flight
To its own likeness, as each mass may bear;
And bursting in its beauty and its might
From trees and beasts and men into the Heavens' light.

The splendours of the firmament of time
May be eclipsed, but are extinguished not;
Like stars to their appointed height they climb,
And death is a low mist which cannot blot
The brightness it may veil. When lofty thought
Lifts a young heart above its mortal lair,
And love and life contend in it, for what
Shall be its earthly doom, the dead live there
And move like winds of light on dark and stormy air.

The inheritors of unfulfilled renown
Rose from their thrones, built beyond mortal thought,
Far in the Unapparent. Chatterton
Rose pale, his solemn agony had not
Yet faded from him; Sidney as he fought

And as he fell and as he lived and loved
Sublimely mild, a Spirit without spot,
Arose; and Lucan, by his death approved:
Oblivion as they rose shrank like a thing reproved.

46

And many more, whose names on Earth are dark,
But whose transmitted effluence cannot die
So long as fire outlives the parent spark,
Rose, robed in dazzling immortality.
'Thou art become as one of us,' they cry,
'It was for thee yon kingless sphere has long
Swung blind in unascended majesty,
Silent alone amid an Heaven of Song.
Assume thy wingèd throne, thou Vesper of our throng!'

47

Who mourns for Adonais? oh, come forth
Fond wretch! and know thyself and him aright,
Clasp with thy panting soul the pendulous Earth;
As from a centre, dart thy spirit's light
Beyond all worlds, until its spacious might
Satiate the void circumference: then shrink
Even to a point within our day and night;
And keep thy heart light lest it make thee sink
When hope has kindled hope, and lured thee to the
    brink;

Or go to Rome, which is the sepulchre,
O, not of him, but of our joy: 'tis nought
That ages, empires, and religions there
Lie buried in the ravage they have wrought;
For such as he can lend, – they borrow not
Glory from those who made the world their prey;
And he is gathered to the kings of thought
Who waged contention with their time's decay,
And of the past are all that cannot pass away.

Go thou to Rome, – at once the Paradise,
The grave, the city, and the wilderness;
And where its wrecks like shattered mountains rise,
And flowering weeds, and fragrant copses dress
The bones of Desolation's nakedness
Pass, till the Spirit of the spot shall lead
Thy footsteps to a slope of green access
Where, like an infant's smile, over the dead,
A light of laughing flowers along the grass is spread.

And grey walls moulder round, on which dull Time
Feeds, like slow fire upon a hoary brand:
And one keen pyramid with wedge sublime,
Pavilioning the dust of him who planned
This refuge for his memory, doth stand

Like flame transformed to marble; and beneath,
A field is spread, on which a newer band
Have pitched in Heaven's smile their camp of death,
Welcoming him we lose with scarce extinguished breath.

51

Here pause: these graves are all too young as yet
To have outgrown the sorrow which consigned
Its charge to each; and if the seal is set,
Here, on one fountain of a mourning mind,
Break it not thou! too surely shalt thou find
Thine own well full, if thou returnest home,
Of tears and gall. From the world's bitter wind
Seek shelter in the shadow of the tomb.
What Adonais is, why fear we to become?

52

The One remains, the many change and pass;
Heaven's light forever shines, Earth's shadows fly;
Life, like a dome of many-coloured glass,
Stains the white radiance of Eternity,
Until Death tramples it to fragments. – Die,
If thou wouldst be with that which thou dost seek!
Follow where all is fled! – Rome's azure sky,
Flowers, ruins, statues, music, words, are weak
The glory they transfuse with fitting truth to speak.

Why linger, why turn back, why shrink, my Heart?
Thy hopes are gone before: from all things here
They have departed; thou shouldst now depart!
A light is passed from the revolving year,
And man, and woman; and what still is dear
Attracts to crush, repels to make thee wither.
The soft sky smiles, – the low wind whispers near:
'Tis Adonais calls! oh, hasten thither,
No more let Life divide what Death can join together.

That Light whose smile kindles the Universe,
That Beauty in which all things work and move,
That Benediction which the eclipsing Curse
Of birth can quench not, that sustaining Love
Which through the web of being blindly wove
By man and beast and earth and air and sea,
Burns bright or dim, as each are mirrors of
The fire for which all thirst, now beams on me,
Consuming the last clouds of cold mortality.

The breath whose might I have invoked in song
Descends on me; my spirit's bark is driven
Far from the shore, far from the trembling throng
Whose sails were never to the tempest given;
The massy earth and spherèd skies are riven!

I am borne darkly, fearfully, afar;
Whilst burning through the inmost veil of Heaven,
The soul of Adonais, like a star,
Beacons from the abode where the Eternal are.

The Flower That Smiles Today

The flower that smiles today
   Tomorrow dies;
All that we wish to stay
   Tempts and then flies;
What is this world's delight?
Lightning, that mocks the night,
   Brief even as bright. –

Virtue, how frail it is! –
   Friendship, how rare! –
Love, how it sells poor bliss
   For proud despair!
But these, though soon they fall,
Survive their joy, and all
   Which ours we call. –

Whilst skies are blue and bright,
   Whilst flowers are gay,
Whilst eyes that change ere night
   Make glad the day;

Whilst yet the calm hours creep,
Dream thou – and from thy sleep
    Then wake to weep.

To Night

Swiftly walk o'er the western wave,
    Spirit of Night!
Out of the misty eastern cave
Where, all the long and lone daylight
Thou wovest dreams of joy and fear,
Which make thee terrible and dear,
    Swift be thy flight!

Wrap thy form in a mantle grey,
    Star-inwrought!
Blind with thine hair the eyes of Day,
Kiss her until she be wearied out –
Then wander o'er city and sea and land,
Touching all with thine opiate wand –
    Come, long-sought!

When I arose and saw the dawn
    I sighed for thee;
When light rode high, and the dew was gone,
And noon lay heavy on flower and tree,
And the weary Day turned to his rest,

Lingering like an unloved guest,
    I sighed for thee.

Thy brother Death came, and cried,
    'Wouldst thou me?'
Thy sweet child Sleep, the filmy-eyed,
Murmured like a noontide bee,
'Shall I nestle near thy side?
Wouldst thou me?' and I replied,
    'No, not thee!'

Death will come when thou art dead,
    Soon, too soon –
    Sleep will come when thou art fled;
Of neither would I ask the boon
I ask of thee, belovèd Night –
Swift be thine approaching flight,
    Come soon, soon!

A Note on Percy Bysshe Shelley

Percy Bysshe Shelley (1792–1822), English poet, born at Field Place, near Horsham, Sussex. He was educated at Sion House School, Isleworth, and at Eton, where he speedily earned a reputation for eccentricity but also showed himself an apt scholar, learning Greek and Latin, and reading omnivorously. Before his schooldays were over he had published two prose romances and, in collaboration with his sister Elizabeth, a book of verse, *Original Poetry, by Victor and Cazire*, 1810. In 1810 he entered University College, Oxford, but soon after matriculating he joined Thomas Jefferson Hogg, the future biographer, in the production of a pamphlet, *The Necessity of Atheism*, 1811, which gave so much offence that he was sent down. Forbidden by his father to come home, he went instead to London. Here he met (characteristically, through trying to rescue her from her father's oppression) Harriet Westbrook, two years younger than himself, with whom he eloped to Edinburgh in 1811.

For a while the couple lived at Keswick, Shelley meanwhile showing himself an ardent revolutionary in politics, championing the various radical movements in Britain and more especially in Ireland (1812). In the following year he published privately *Queen Mab*, and came under the influence of the radical William Godwin. At this time he and his wife drifted apart, and in spring 1814 Shelley eloped again – to Switzerland with Godwin's daughter Mary. This action accorded with his view of marriage as an artificial and degrading restraint, and he appeared surprised when like-minded friends nevertheless condemned his conduct. In 1816 Harriet drowned herself. Shelley then married Mary Godwin, issued the memorable *Alastor*, and also travelled in Switzerland and France. Returning to England, he became reconciled to his father, who settled on him a small but adequate income; and after living for some time at Marlow, and then near Windsor, Shelley and his wife proceeded to Italy. Here they led a wandering life, saddened by the death of an infant son and daughter, but in 1820 they finally settled at Pisa.

His contact with Italy was a landmark in Shelley's intellectual development. Here he composed *The Cenci*, 1819, 'Ode to the West Wind', 1819, *Rosalind and Helen*, 1819, and *Prometheus Unbound*, 1820; while at Pisa he wrote many of his finest short lyrics, and also *Epipsychidion*, 1821, *Adonais*, 1821, his elegy on the death of Keats, and *Hellas*, 1822. He continued to champion the cause of freedom in England and Italy, while he read Greek literature incessantly, mastered Spanish, Italian, and German, and translated Calderon, Dante, and Goethe. From Pisa he went to Ravenna to stay with Byron, whose acquaintance he had made some years before. In July 1822, while sailing to Specia, his boat foundered in a storm and he was drowned. After many days his body was found by his friend Edward Trelawny, who cremated it on the seashore, with Byron among the mourners. The ashes were taken to Rome and interred in the Protestant cemetery which Shelley himself had described as a place so lovely that 'it might make one in love with death'.

Shelley is often pictured as an ethereal visionary. This view fails to take account of his development from the over-simplified theories of his youth, his great learning, or his readiness to risk involvement with the pain and injustice of the world. In *A Defence of Poetry*, written in 1821, but unpublished until 1840, Shelley declared his belief in poetry as a moral force: 'The greatest instrument of moral good is the imagination; and poetry administers to the effect by acting upon the cause'. Many of his poems were radical and reforming in aim; but, though these excited much contemporary interest and contain stirring passages (such as his eulogies on freedom in *Hellas*), Shelley is chiefly remembered as one of the greatest lyric poets. His experiments in poetic drama (apart from *The Cenci*) and his political hymns are insignificant beside such masterpieces as the 'Ode to the West Wind', 'The Cloud', and 'To a Skylark'.